IDOLS OF
K-POP

Your
Must-Have Guide
to Who's Who

ISBN 978-0-06-297778-6

Typography by Rick Farley
19 20 21 22 23 PC/LSCW 10 9 8 7 6 5 4 3 2 1

First U.S. edition, 2019
Originally published in Great Britain in 2019 by Dean, an imprint of
Egmont UK Limited.

IDOLS OF
K-POP

Your Must-Have Guide to Who's Who

Malcolm Mackenzie

HARPER
An Imprint of HarperCollinsPublishers

10

22

She has aegyo, but do you know who else does?

BTS is on page 10 and 12, 17, 20, 22—you get the idea.

30

Here are two members of NCT—turn to page 30 for the other 900.

36

Steady yourselves, it's EXO.

54

Is it hot in here or is it just Wanna One?

TWICE has tons of talent.

48

PAGING DR. POP

CONTENTS

18 Find SEVENTEEN on page 18. Awkward, aren't we?

If you like Red Velvet, you'll love Victoria Sponge.

58

KOREA ADVISER

K-pop doesn't just pop—it explodes like a confetti cannon!

The first time you experience K-pop, it seems like a lot, like A LOT, but when you snap back to reality, everything is drab by comparison: slow, predictable, and BORING. The pop music coming out of the South Korean capital, Seoul, is a juggernaut of exuberance— once heard, never forgotten. It devours references from everywhere, feeding them into the K-pop meglo-machine—until something astonishing emerges, shining like the future. That in a nutshell is BTS, TWICE, and EXO, and all the bands that cannot be contained by lowercase letters.

GENERATION NATION

K-pop is roughly split into three, four, or five generations depending on how pedantic you are.

● **The first generation** kick-started with Seo Taiji and Boys in 1992, gathering momentum, but staying relatively confined to Korea with the likes of H.O.T. and S.E.S.

● **The second-generation** artists like Girls' Generation, Super Junior, and Big Bang went mainstream pop and started to have massive hits all over Asia in the mid-2000s. This was the beginning of the "Hallyu Wave."

● **The third generation** came around 2010 with idol groups 2NE1, SHINee, SISTAR, and Psy.

● **The fourth generation** probably emerged around 2015, when slick artists like EXO, BLACKPINK, TWICE, Red Velvet, and of course BTS started killing it globally. ***This is not science, people—it's just a fun debate***

Jennie (BLACKPINK) represents the 4th generation of K-pop (or is it the 5th? Or the 3rd?).

Trainees say: "Pick me!"

Unlike the UK and US business models, where managers and record companies put together bands because they look nice and can hold a tune, in Korea wannabe pop stars typically audition for special companies (SM, JYP, YG, etc.) that train them for years on how to sing and dance and basically become flawless entertainers. Only the very best will launch as idols.

Trainees vie for a position in girl group IZ*ONE on the TV show *Produce 48*.

ROLE PLAY

If you thought Baby, Scary, Sporty, Ginger, and Posh nailed it in terms of the roles you can play in a vocal group, brace yourself for K-pop's list of who-does-what.

Main vocalist: arguably the best singer with the greatest vocal range—sings the chorus.
Lead vocalist: another great singer who often starts and ends the song.
Sub-vocalists: the other singers who fill in the gaps.
Main rapper: the best rapper in the band, who will get most of the rap parts.
Lead rapper: the next most talented rapper.
Sub-rappers: the back up rappers.

Main dancer: the best dancer in the band.
Lead dancer: the next most talented dancer.
Leader: the one who leads and represents the group.
Maknae: the youngest.
Visual: the most typically attractive member according to Korean beauty ideals.
Center: the one who tends to be in the middle.
Face: the member who's most popular.

Idols can have one role or many roles, and sometimes even switch roles.

LEAD DANCER VOCALIST

LEAD RAPPER

VOCALIST VISUAL

MAIN VOCALIST LEAD DANCER SUB-RAPPER CENTER MAKNAE

LEADER MAIN RAPPER

MAIN DANCER LEAD VOCALIST

MAIN DANCER RAPPER SUB-VOCALIST

BTS

LET'S UNPACK K-POP

Take a deep dive into 11 things that make K-pop tick.

1 Agencies

In most countries, record labels run the music industry. In South Korea, it's a whole other ball-game—y'know, like Quidditch except with billions of dollars. Monolithic companies (SM, JM, Cube, JYP, Big Hit) exist to train kids and turn them into stars, a bit like the old studio system in Hollywood, except way tougher— Lassie had it easy.

2 Bulletproof Boy Scouts

BTS has single-handedly (14-handedly?) changed the game. Not just for K-pop but how we think about music. Suddenly songs in a different language don't seem strange. BTS doesn't just mean Bulletproof Boy Scouts, it means BUSINESS.

3 Capital letters

ABCDE

The names of groups and idols are a cocktail of capital letters. Sometimes it's a full word like WINNER, an acronym like BTS, or a single letter like HyunA. Capital letters are powerful and strong with all their sharp edges and shouty attitude, plus this stylistic choice makes the words easier to read.

4 Dance routines

American boy bands and girl bands have tended to scrape by on charisma. They might've bopped about or had a few "routines" but jaw-dropping dancers like Kai (EXO), Jimin (BTS), or Momo (TWICE) have the skills of Maddie Ziegler, and it's ONLY one part of what they do.

5 English

K-pop is from Korea, so of course it's sung in Korean, but why does it feature a bunch of English words? Probably because English is a pervasive language in popular culture and just sounds cool.

EXO are the kings of choreo. The M/V for "Tempo" is just flawless.

6 Frequency

K-pop artists follow the little-and-often rule, releasing content on the regular and mixing up formats to keep things fresh. In 2018 alone, TWICE released two EPs including the killer *What Is Love*, a revamped album *Summer Nights*, super-kawaii Japanese album *BDZ*, six addicting singles, and eight glorious videos.

7 Gender challenging

They wear makeup, have hair like cotton candy, and aren't afraid to express their emotions: welcome to the world of male idols. These boys could have come straight from Lisa Simpson's beloved *Non-Threatening Boys* magazine, and that's part of their appeal—they're polite, pretty, and totally relatable.

In M/Vs like "Idol," BTS challenges norms of masculinity with glee.

8 Happiness TM

K-pop sells pure joy. The songs are bright and exciting, the M/Vs are a feast for the senses, and the talent, ambition, and commitment make us gasp.

HyunA [center] and E'Dawn [right] have dated for years.

9 Image

Pop stars like Justin Bieber seem to do what they want and remain popular, but idols are expected to be perfect on- and offstage. When HyunA revealed she'd been dating PENTAGON member E'Dawn in 2018, they were both "let go." These exacting standards highlight a darker side to K-pop that Western fans must wrestle with.

10 Japan

The biggest early adopter and continuing supporter of K-pop is Japan. It's become such big business that idol groups regularly record entire albums in Japanese. And it's no wonder the Japanese love K-pop; it takes plenty of inspiration from Japanese culture.

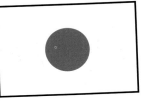

11 Korean wave

Hallyu is not the catchphrase of Shangela from *RuPaul's Drag Race*, it's the Korean Wave. That is, the spreading of Korean culture to the world. K-pop is a massive part of that, peaking with Psy's record-breaking "Gangnam Style" and skyrocketing with BTS.

Psy's horsey dance was a turning point.

RM
Full name:
Kim Nam-joon
Role: Leader, main rapper

JIMIN
Full name:
Park Ji-min
Role: Main dancer, lead vocalist

V
Full name:
Kim Tae-hyung
Role: Lead dancer, vocalist

LOVE YOURSELF 轉

JIN
Full name:
Kim Seok-jin
Role: Vocalist, visual

J-HOPE
Full name:
Jung Ho-seok
Role: Main dancer, rapper, sub-vocalist

Full name:
Jeon Jungkook
Role: Main vocalist, lead dancer, sub-rapper, center, maknae

JUNGKOOK

SUGA
Full name:
Min Yoon-gi
Role: Lead rapper

방탄소년단

BTS

Right now it looks like BTS really is bulletproof.

THE JOURNEY

BTS was formed by Big Hit Entertainment in 2010, but was officially launched in the summer of 2013.

Surprisingly, their first single, raucous rallying cry "No More Dream," wasn't a huge hit, but the tide soon changed. With refreshingly frank lyrics and tunes they largely wrote and produced themselves, BTS was a boyband that felt "real." Their dedicated interaction with fans sent the boys' popularity stratospheric, and now BTS snatches trophies and breaks records for breakfast. Nom.

BURN THE STAGE

In 2018 BTS smashed One Direction's record for biggest opening weekend of a concert film with *Burn the Stage: The Movie* taking $14 million!!!

BREAKDOWN

The band's name takes many forms. In the UK and US, BTS stands for Beyond The Scene. In Korea, they are Bangtan Boys or Bangtan Sonyeondan, which roughly translates to Bulletproof Boy Scouts, while in Japan, it's Bōdan Shōnen-dan.

SWIFT EXIT

Taylor Swift's YouTube record for most views in 24 hours was smashed by BTS's super-saturated M/V for "IDOL," which had 45 million—two million more than Tay-Tay's "Look What You Made Me Do."

SWEET CHARITY

BTS was the first K-pop group to speak at the United Nations.

UNITING NATIONS

UNICEF isn't a rookie idol group—it's a massive children's charity, and they chose BTS as ambassadors to launch their Love Myself campaign. Google RM's speech—it's brilliant.

BTS

"The [US] tour was unforgettable. Personally, my favorite moments were when I went to MoMA [Museum of Modern Art] in NY and the Chicago art museum."
V is v, v arty.

"I'm pretty cheerful, but I don't really like noisiness."
Suga asks you to scream softly.

"It's still hard to believe it's happening. It's like a dream."
No, you're like a dream, Jin. *dreams of Jin for 30 minutes*

"I guess the music, the lyrics, our passion, and I think our sincerity goes across those barriers."
Jungkook on why BTS transcends language.

"I have many faults and I have many more fears, but I'm going to embrace myself as hard as I can. And I'm starting to love myself gradually, just little by little."
RM speaking for just about all of us there.

"V sometimes acts like a brat, but in our eyes, he's still really cute. So, I can't help but look after him."
Need some help, Jimin?

"Everyone liked me when I went up on the stage at a talent search in elementary school, and that's when I decided to become a music artist."
The lesson from J-Hope: keep twerking and werkin'.

LEARN THE LANGUAGE OF K-POP

The number of people learning Korean is on the rise, but if you don't have the time, chill, we got you. The essentials of K-pop terminology are here. Boom! Or should that be LABOUM?

Put away your baes, huns, and OMGs—there's some new slang in town.

Aegyo
Acting cute and making the fans melt.

Antis
The people who hate a particular idol group.

Beagle
Playful and energetic idols—like the dog.

Bias
The idols who you love more than others are your bias. Your No. 1 is your Absolute Bias. When your faves change, that can be a Bias Wrecker.

The Big Three
Three entertainment companies: SM, YG, and JYP.

Bogoshipo
"I miss you."

Chingu
Friend.

Co-ed group
Idol group with boys and girls like KARD and Triple H.

Daebak
When something is amazing, a bit like "Wow."

Daesang
The grand prize at the Seoul Music Awards.

Flower Boy (kkonminam)
A gentle, pretty boy as opposed to a bad boy.

Gaon Music Chart
The official Korean music chart that started in 2010.

Hallyu
The Korean Wave of performing arts sweeping the world.

Hanbok
The traditional Korean national dress.

Hoobae
Someone younger or less experienced.

Hwaiting
Encouraging term, like "Go for it!"

Hyung
Big brother—it's what younger boys call older boys.

Idols
What all of the pop stars of South Korea are called.

Jagiya
Term of endearment like babe or bae.

Kyeopta
"That's cute."

Line/Liners
Idols that share a commonality are on a . . . line, e.g.: Baekhyun Chen and Chanyeol are "Beagle liners."

Maknae
The youngest member of a group.

M/V
Music video.

Netizen
Internet + citizen = someone on the internet.

Noona, Nuna
Big sister, used by boys to a girl who is older than them.

Omona
An exclamation of surprise like, "Oh my gosh!" Omo for short.

Oopa
What a girl might call an older boy or man.

Pepero Day
November 11 is a day where loved ones exchange chocolate-dipped bread sticks, "Peperos." A bit like Valentine's Day.

Rookie
Newly launched idol group or solo idol.

Sarang
Love.

Saranghae
I love you.

Sasaeng
Obsessive fan.

Selca
Selfie.

Sunbae
Someone older or more experienced.

Trainee
Someone signed to an entertainment company but has yet to be launched.

Unnie
What a younger girl calls an older girl.

Weekly Idol
A variety TV show where idols regularly appear.

White Day
March 14—a month after Valentine's Day, when boys give gifts to girls, often white chocolate.

Yeh
Yes.

meet the
MAKNAE

Nobody puts baby in the corner, at least not in K-pop.

Everyone loves babies, so it should come as no surprise that the baby of K-pop idol groups holds a special place in the hearts of their bands and fans. The maknae is often the mischievous, naughty one who brings LOLs, excitement, and energy to the group. Being the youngest means that sometimes they're shy and quiet while at other times they're loud and uncontrollable, but one thing's for sure: they are always totally lovable.

Sehun EXO

Sehun might be the most popular maknae in the world. At the time of writing he had 14.6 million followers on Instagram—that's more than the population of Seoul. According to the editor of *Vogue Korea*, his eye-catching cover in August 2018 was the biggest selling since it launched in 1996. Cute in more ways than one.

EVIL MAKNAE

Don't panic, it's not as bad as it sounds—it just means teasing and being super annoying. Yeri has been branded "Evil Maknae" for her wicked sense of humor, and sometimes she's accused of being too savage, but having an outspoken member in a girl group is a total bonus.

FAKE MAKNAE

Fake maknaes are the idols that look very young and are often mistaken for the baby of the group. Some might take this as an insult, but surely it's much better than being told you look haggard, right? Nayeon from TWICE is the ultimate Fake Maknae, which can annoy some antis.

JIN

JUNGKOOK

Jin (BTS) has been given the nickname MADNAE because he likes to goof around like a big kid.

Jungkook BTS

Jungkook's nickname is "the Golden Maknae" because he may be the youngest BTSer, but he has incredible talents as well as cheeks you want to pinch. Word is, he was one of the most sought-after trainees of all time, and when you see him sing and dance, it's easy to understand why he's so precious.

Lisa BLACKPINK

She may be the maknae, but Thai rap goddess Lisa showed she was no pushover when she swapped her glamorous life to appear in hard-core military reality TV show *Real Men 300*. She did have a little cry, though—you can take the baby out of the band . . . etc.

막내미 뚜두뚜두
리 사
진짜사나이
300
2018.09
coming soon

세븐틴

SEVENTEEN

There aren't 17 of them, don't panic—13 is plenty.

TEEN PLAYERS

Pledis Entertainment introduced the boys in 2013 with an online streaming show called *SEVENTEEN TV*, and they became a bona fide group in 2015 with their first EP, *17 Carat*—the longest-charting K-pop album in the US. Their second EP, *Boys Be*, was the biggest-selling rookie record of the same year in Korea.

UNITS UNITE

Because they're such a big group, SEVENTEEN is split into the three units—**Hip-Hop:** S.Coups, Wonwoo, Mingyu, Vernon; **Vocal:** Jeonghan, Joshua, Woozi, DK, Seungkwan; **Performance:** Jun, Hoshi, The8, and Dino—with each member specializing in one of those three areas.

The rap line clicks.

DIYDOLS

SEVENTEEN has written and produced most of their own songs since their debut album, *Love & Letter*. Woozi has also penned tunes for I.O.I and Ailee.

SEVENTEEN TV

TV TIMES

SEVENTEEN TV lasted for five seasons while they searched for the perfect combo. With that much content, it's no surprise people fell in love with them.

24-CARAT FANS

"It's amazing when overseas fans try to speak to us in Korean," admits Joshua. "We're thankful and blessed at their effort to learn a different language just to converse with us."

PILLOWS 2 GO

M/Vs are precisely choreographed, so SEVENTEEN was thrilled to have a pillow fight for the "OH MY!" video. "It felt like I was playing with friends on a school trip," said DK.

SQUAD GOALS

JUN
Full name: Wen Jun-whi
Role: Lead dancer, sub-vocalist

DINO
Full name: Lee Chan
Role: Main dancer, sub-vocalist, lead rapper, maknae

THE8
Full name: Xu Minghao
Role: Lead dancer, sub-vocalist, rapper

HOSHI
Full name: Kwon Soon-young
Role: Leader (Performance unit), main dancer, lead vocalist, sub-rapper

Performance unit

JEONGHAN
Full name: Yoon Jeonghan
Role: Lead vocalist

SEUNGKWAN
Full name: Boo Seung-kwan
Role: Main vocalist

DK
Full name: Lee Seokmin
Role: Main vocalist

WOOZI
Full name: Lee Jihoon
Role: Leader (Vocal unit), lead vocalist

JOSHUA
Full name: Joshua Hong
Role: Lead vocalist

Vocal unit

WONWOO
Full name: Jeon Wonwoo
Role: Lead rapper, sub-vocalist

VERNON
Full name: Hansol Vernon Choi
Role: Main rapper, vocalist

S.COUPS
Full name: Choi Sung-cheol
Role: Leader and leader of the Hip-Hop unit, main rapper, vocalist

MINGYU
Full name: Kim Mingyu
Role: Lead rapper, sub-vocalist, visual, face

Hip-Hop unit

K-POP BY

Glasses at the ready, fact fans—here comes the science bit . . .

1992
The year Seo Taiji and Boys launched, kick-starting the K-pop industry

12.4 MILLION
The number of US streams of BLACK-PINK's "Ddu-Du Ddu-Du" in the first week of release

6'1"
Height of Mingyu (SEVENTEEN), one of the tallest K-pop idols

2:48
Length of Jennie (BLACKPINK)'s "Solo" in minutes and seconds

430,000
Number of people who saw *BTS Live Trilogy Episode III: The Wings Tour*

10 YEARS
Length of time TWICE idol Jihyo spent training before she made her debut

$40 MILLION
Amount Big Bang's G-Dragon is reportedly worth

4 MONTHS
Amount of training EXO's Baekhyun underwent before appearing with the band

30 MILLION
Number of digital singles Girls' Generation has sold

10
The number of countries GFriend topped the iTunes chart in in 2018 with their mini-album *Time for the Moon Night*

14
The age of Lisa (BLACKPINK) when she auditioned for YG

8
The age difference in years between Taeil and Jisung, the oldest and youngest members of NCT

17 CARAT
The debut album of SEVENTEEN

NUMBERS

$4.7 BILLION
The amount the K-pop industry made in 2016

1,793
The number of days it took BTS to get 10 million followers on Twitter—more than any other Korean artist ever

23
The number of number one hit songs G-Dragon has written or cowritten on the Korean Gaon Digital Chart

9
The number of weeks "Gee" by Girls' Generation stayed at number one on the *Music Bank* TV show in 2009, the most ever until Psy's "Gangnam Style"

90,000
The number of signatures a fan petition in support of HyunA and E'Dawn's relationship got after their fallout with Cube Entertainment

$500,000
The amount 2NE1's M/V "Come Back Home" is said to have cost

100 MILLION
"Gee" by Girls' Generation was the first song by a K-pop girl group to exceeed 100 million views on YouTube

630%
The sales increase in China of a shampoo brand when Super Junior mentioned it on a reality show in 2015

14.6 MILLION
The number of followers Sehun (EXO) has on Instagram, making him the most popular maknae on Insta

252,200
The number of retweets a tweet by BTS gets on average

45 MILLION
Number of views of BTS's "Idol" on YouTube in the first 24 hours: a record

1,104,617
Number of pre-orders for EXO's album *Don't Mess Up My Tempo*—their highest ever

16
The number of girls that fought for one of the nine spots in TWICE on the TV show *Sixteen*

10 OF THE BEST
AEGYO

Clasp your hands and prepare for annihilation by cuteness.

"Aegyo" means acting cute and adorable on purpose because you got game, but are a big softie underneath it all. Some of the popular gimmicks idols pull out of the bag are: lip biting, baby voices, winking, blowing kisses, and, most common of all, hand and finger gestures that form heart shapes and peace signs. Most groups indulge in the cheesy guilty pleasure—look . . .

BTOB
Heart-mouth?
Okay, sure, why not?

Weki Meki
Present face—like a flower in full bloom.

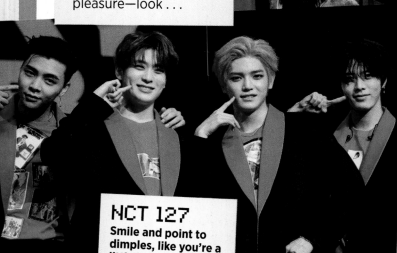

NCT 127
Smile and point to dimples, like you're a little baby—goo goo.

BTS
"V for victory" is more cool than cute, especially when your name is V.

WANNA ONE
Love-heart hands show the fans that you care.

INFINITE
Peace out, man—but not in that hat.

MAMAMOO
David Attenborough says heart-swan hands mate for life.

APINK
Who doesn't love the "pointy fingers, knee-jerk rinky-dink wink"?

MONSTA X
Have trouble expressing aegyo? Choose mini thumb/finger hearts.

MOMOLAND
Giant heart of arms—this is getting silly now.

LISA

Full name:
Lalisa Manoban
Role: Main dancer, lead rapper, sub-vocalist, maknae

JISOO

Full name:
Kim Ji Soo
Role: Lead vocalist, visual

JENNIE

Full name:
Jennie Kim
Role: Main rapper, lead vocalist, center

ROSÉ

Full name:
Park Chae Young
English name:
Roseanne Park
Role: Main vocalist, lead dancer

블랙핑크

BLACKPINK

Badda bing badda boom, BLACKPINK in the room.

'As If It's Your Last" would NOT be their last M/V to break records.

STARS ARE BORN

BLACKPINK has the world shook. In 2016 YG Entertainment took a gamble on launching their first girl group since 2NE1, and it paid off spectacularly. Their first two singles went to number one and two on the Billboard world digital chart, the fastest K-pop group to ever do this. Aside from badass songs, immaculate visuals, and slick M/Vs, BP are cooler than Canada.

BLACK+PINK = BIG THINK

The band's name has multiple meanings: the "pink" encapsulates their girly side and the "black" stands for strength and power.

BLACKPINK

DDU DU

How could the girls' signature song not be a hit? It's a bop! It got to number 55 in the US chart, the highest ever for a K-pop girl group.

DUA LOOPY

BLACKPINK is the first female K-pop idol group to enter the UK Top 40. Their version of "Kiss and Make Up" with Dua Lipa entered the chart at number 36.

NEED A LEADER?

Unlike most bands, BLACKPINK doesn't have a leader. Because the quartet became such good friends during training, they didn't want to mess up the dynamic with a bossy-pants leader.

COOL IT

KEEPING UP WITH THE BLINKS

In 2018 BLACKPINK got their very own 12-part reality show, BLACKPINK House. If you haven't already, watch it on YouTube and marvel at their fear of cushions and balloons.

BLACKPINK

"Our fans from all around the world: we are so grateful for the love and support."
Jisoo thanks you.

"We would love to have any opportunities that we can to perform in front of you guys, not just in Korea, maybe one day in front of everyone around the world."
If you could come to the US that would be great, Jennie.

"I search for music I like or interviews by artists I like on YouTube. I think watching those videos has a healing effect."
YouTube takes Rosé to her happy place.

"We are incredibly happy people because we are doing what we love."
Lucky for us that Lisa's love is our love.

all eyes on the
VISUAL

Not just a pretty face—the arms and abs are decent as well.

Sometimes when you discover the official visual of a group, it can be baffling, but everyone has a special appeal, so let's just appreciate the "visuals" of K-pop's most eye-catching male idols.

Cha Eun-woo
ASTRO
The group is pretty good, but their visual is straight up pretty.

L INFINITE
Kim Myung-soo is so handsome he became an actor, because of course he did.

Mingyu
SEVENTEEN
He's friends with fellow 97-liner Jungkook—imagine double dating with those two . . .

Jin BTS

V is regularly voted one of the best-looking men on the planet, but that doesn't stop Jin from being Worldwide Handsome—mwah!

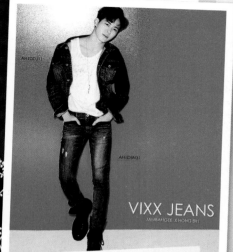

VIXX JEANS

Hongbin VIXX

When VIXX was asked to launch and model a range of cool jeans for Jambangee, Hongbin nailed the assignment.

Mark GOT7

Mark sings to a teddy bear in his atmospheric solo M/V "Nobody Knows"—er, dude KNOWS exactly what he's doing.

Kai EXO

EXO is a group of visuals, but we wouldn't trade Kai for anyone else.

Siwon SUPER JUNIOR

When Siwon finally finished his military service, he stood to attention and so did everyone else.

JUNGWOO

Full name:
Kim Jung-woo
Role: Lead vocalist,
lead dancer

MARK

JOHNNY

Full name:
Mark Lee
Role: Main rapper,
vocalist

YUTA

DOYOUNG

Full name:
Seo Young-ho
Role: Lead rapper,
lead dancer, vocalist

Full name:
Nakamoto Yuta
Role: Main dancer,
rapper, vocalist

Full name:
Kim Dong-young
Role: Main vocalist

WINWIN

Full name:
Dong Si-cheng
Role: Lead dancer,
vocalist

HAECHAN

Full name:
Lee Dong-hyuck
Role: Lead vocalist,
lead dancer, sub-rapper,
maknae

TAEYONG

Full name:
Lee Tae-yong
Role: Leader, main
dancer, main rapper,
vocalist, visual, center

JAEHYUN

Full name:
Jung Yoon-oh
Role: Lead vocalist,
lead dancer, rapper

TAEIL

Full name:
Moon Tae-il
Role: Main vocalist

NCT 127

Watch them take over the world with technology.

WE ARE FAMILY

NCT 127 is just part of the NCT Family, which currently stands at 18 members and includes 4 subunits: NCT 127, NCT Dream, NCT U, and WayV (based in China). Members blend between units, so you need to pay careful attention to who does what where. NCT has been in their infancy since 2013, but NCT 127 launched in 2016 and is already slaying the game.

WAY BIG

This many members in an idol group is anything but regular.

FINDING NEO

According to SM Entertainment, NCT stands for Neo Culture Technology—which means delivering Korean culture to the entire world—while 127 is the longitudinal coordinate for Seoul, the capital of South Korea.

SEOUL

NCT USA

NCT 127 was another US success story in 2018. Their inventive, eclectic debut album *Regular-Irregular* got to 86 on the Billboard chart, and they were even nominated for a Teen Choice Award.

COMEBACK KIDS

When the band came back in with the *Limitless* EP in January 2017, they delivered two new band members: Johnny and Doyoung, while for *Regular-Irregular* the following year, Jungwoo joined the group. Better than a bonus instrumental.

DREAM ON

NCT Dream is the junior unit with a sweeter bubblegum sound—as evidenced by their apty titled debut single. To keep the band young and fresh, whenever anyone turns 19 they will have to leave the band. Way harsh, Tai.

YOU KNOW IT'S K-POP WHEN . . .

K-pop is not clichéd—it just knows what it likes, okay?

Chandeliers seem to be everywhere.

Everything is hyper-saturated, clashing, and glitching—as the sun goes down.

Everyone took their style inspiration from macarons and My Little Pony.

THE MUSIC CUTS OUT FOR A FRACTION OF A SECOND AND SLAMS BACK IN.

The name of the band sounds like obscure text-speak or a government scheme for weekend parking. Maybe that's why everyone seems to be in a parking lot.

THE BOYS HAVE BETTER EYELINER THAN YOU.

Suddenly there's a shopping cart, a washing machine, a flying car, and cheese balls—what is this strange place?

Someone is inexplicably in a bath . . . clothed.

THERE ARE ENOUGH PEOPLE TO START A LACROSSE TEAM.

You've listened to the song five times and you still only know four words and they're "La, la, la, la."

It sounds like you're in the sixties, then a shoot-'em-up game, then an Ibiza trance club, then a nursery school.

There's a level of dancing that would make Dance Moms's Abby Lee book a flight to sign up the talent.

Gender identity is as blurry as a net curtain.

ADULTS ARE WEARING SCHOOL UNIFORMS AND EATING LOLLIPOPS.

You're either in an airy room with white light streaming through the windows or a dark, neon-lit alleyway.

The song has a title that's an attention-grabbing noise, like: Peek-A-Boo, Go Go, Wee Woo, Whistle, Growl, Clap, Freeze, Baam, Danger, Siren, Hoot, Knock Knock, Beep Beep.

6 sassy
GIRLS
GROUPS

Welcome to the . . .

Gee, Gee, Gee, Gee Generation.

SUMMER FUN with THE WONDER GIRLS

MTV | IGGY

WONDER GIRLS

The JYP-signed group debuted the same year as SNSD as part of the second generation of K-pop groups. They toured with the Jonas Brothers, released an album in English, and had their own MTV reality show that ran for four seasons. Their funky retro sound captured hearts and ears everywhere and possibly even inspired Girls Aloud's number one hit "The Promise."

COSMIC GIRLS

Also known as WJSN, these relative rookies are 13 girls with out of this world M/Vs to match their cosmic sound. If you can't find a bias here, you might need to see a doctor.

BROWN EYED GIRLS

If this quartet had only released the glorious "Abracadabra," they'd still deserve a spot on this list. JeA, Miryo, Narsha, and Gain had more attitude than just about anyone, and to prove it they invented the iconic "arrogant dance" that Psy borrowed for his "Gentleman" M/V.

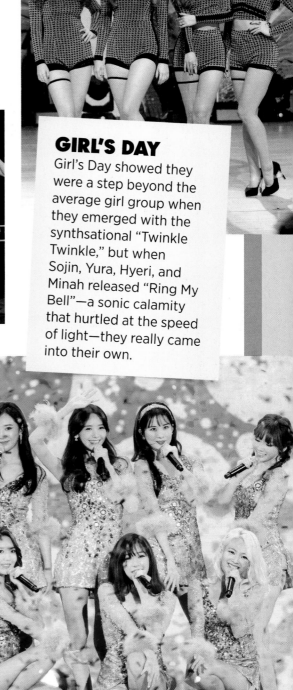

OH MY GIRL

Launched in 2015, the seven-strong group, led by Hyojung, have turned into a total dream. From their eye-catching artwork to transportive tunes on beguiling mini-albums like *Remember Me,* they provide a much-needed escape from the everyday.

GIRL'S DAY

Girl's Day showed they were a step beyond the average girl group when they emerged with the synthsational "Twinkle Twinkle," but when Sojin, Yura, Hyeri, and Minah released "Ring My Bell"—a sonic calamity that hurtled at the speed of light—they really came into their own.

GIRLS' GENERATION

The OG superstars have been called "the Nation's Girl Group" because they're basically Korea's Spice Girls. They had mega success ten years ago and the members, Sunny, Yuri, Taeyeon, Tiffany, Yoona, Seohyun, Sooyoung, Hyoyeon, and Jessica (who left in 2014), are household names. The band, also known as SNSD in their homeland, created an irresistible brand of electro-bubblegum that gave birth to virtually every girl group since, becoming one of K-pop's most successful exports with over a billion streams and YouTube views.

KAI

Full name:
Kim Jong-in
Role: Main dancer,
lead rapper, vocalist,
visual, center

SUHO

Full name:
Kim Jun-myeon
Role: Leader,
lead vocalist

BAEKHYUN

Full name:
Byun Baek-hyun
Role: Main vocalist

CHEN

Full name:
Kim Jong-dae
Role: Main vocalist

D.O.

Full name:
Do Kyung-soo
Role: Main vocalist

CHANYEOL

Full name:
Park Chan-yeol
Role: Main rapper,
vocalist

SEHUN

Full name:
Oh Se-hun
Role: Lead dancer,
lead rapper, sub-
vocalist, maknae

XIUMIN

Full name:
Kim Min-seok
Role: Lead vocalist,
lead dancer, rapper

엑소

EXO

They have the power. Excitement is your only option.

ENTER EXO

EXO burst onto the scene in 2012 c/o SM Entertainment. There were 12 members then, but after a switcheroo or two or four, there are now eight/nine members. Chinese idols Kris, Luhan, and Tao left, while Lay has been laying low working on solo projects. EXO was an instant hit, selling over a million copies of their first album *XOXO*. Since then, each of their five albums has sold over a million and they even made it into the 2018 *Guinness World Records* for most Daesang wins—EXO-llent.

COMIC RELIEF

How do you encourage people to buy a physical copy of your album? Release it with a beautiful graphic novel and a set of collectable trading cards, like EXO did for *THE WAR: The Power of Music*, that's how.

STYLE IT OUT

Supreme, Balenciaga, Vetements, Céline, Saint Laurent, Gosha—wearing labels like these, it's no wonder Vogue.com hailed EXO as the most stylish K-pop band ever.

OLYMPIC TORCH SONGS

The 2018 Winter Olympics in Pyeongchang was watched by billions around the world and EXO was chosen to perform their songs "Power" and "Growl" at the closing ceremony.

KAI & CO

Iconic: "Ko Ko Bop" has nearly 200 million views on YouTube.

KO KO HOT

In 2017 their reggae tinged mega-hit "Ko Ko Bop" had more hashtag mentions on Twitter than any other song. They also took the win for most popular celebs to join Twitter in 2017.

EXO

"There are so many shoes in our dormitory. When packages are delivered to our dorm, the delivery guy always looks surprised by the amount of shoes on the floor."
Chanyeol on the perks and peeves of EXO having multiple shoe endorsements.

"I was a quiet student in school. I didn't want people to know that I was training at SM, so I didn't tell anybody. I just spent my high school years [working] quietly and then I graduated."
Turns out D.O. really is a doer.

"Hearing the name Jong-in while I work is a bit awkward at times but it makes me feel good."
Kai, don't worry about it—Drake is shook when people call him Aubrey.

"[I liked] the military-inspired style in the "Monster" video. It looked a bit more manly, it was comfortable, and the clothes were oversized, which made them easy to dance in."
Do you think Suho is over pastels?

"We took a day trip and played while eating clams and giving the seagulls shrimp snacks."
Sehun recalls a favorite summer memory from his early days in EXO.

"I don't go out much. I spend a lot of my time with my cat. I am really busy with my cat."
Xiumin says "Hello Kitty"— daily .

"We always make sure we have fresh underwear."
Baekhyun reveals EXO's number one travel essential.

"I have never been fully satisfied when I listen to what I have recorded. I still have a long way to go."
Don't be so hard on yourself, Chen.

BOSSI

Who's the daddy in K-pop? These guys.

Jihyo
TWICE

She may not be the oldest, but Jihyo was chosen by TWICE to be their leader after boss JYP told the girls that the ideal leader needs to be a good role model and make sacrifices for the good of the band, and Jihyo fit the bill.

JIHYO

Suho
EXO

It's not easy being the dad of the group, but somehow Suho keeps his EXO beagles and maknae in check and makes sure everyone knows what they're doing. "I've never regretted being a part of EXO as the leader," he said in 2016. "Even if I was reborn, I'd want to be a member of EXO again."

RM
BTS

RM isn't just an amazing group leader—he's pretty much the face of K-pop across the world. *He's* the one charming the pants off talk show hosts when the BTS juggernaut cruises into town, triggering tear ducts with his speeches and going above and beyond to learn English with Phoebe, Joey, and Chandler.

NG IT

Solar
MAMAMOO

The secret to Solar's success as the leader of Mamamoo is addressing an issue as it arises. Now the four can communicate with just a look. "As the leader, if the group members are uncomfortable about something, I act as our representative," she reveals.

Taeyong
NCT 127

If Jungkook is the Golden Maknae, then Taeyong is the golden leader—he does everything short of making the beds. "He definitely has a charisma that comes with being the leader—he acts as the pillar of the group," gushed Yuta.

Onew
SHINee

A recent poll of 200,000 Koreans through music channel Mnet chose RM as the best leader in K-pop—of course—but Onew (SHINee) came in second with 70,000 votes. Onew showed courage and strength following the suicide of bandmate Jonghyun in 2017.

빅뱅

BIGBANG

10 million YouTube subscribers can't be wrong.

PROPER BANGERS

BIGBANG chose their name well. Their impact on Korean music is immeasurable. Since their debut in 2006 the outlandish, innovative, and funny five have blurred

the lines of hip-hop, pop, rock, and fashion to become one of the most exciting acts in the world. In 2016 *Forbes* named them the 13th biggest celebrity earners under 30; ten places above Ed Sheeran—the A-Team indeed.

ATTEN-SHUN

They may be one of the biggest K-pop groups in the world, but that

Feeling the fatigue in *BIGBANG Made: The Movie.*

doesn't mean BIGBANG can escape South Korea's compulsory military service—and that's what four of the five members are doing right now. G-Dragon received so much fan mail it slowed operations.

AB FAB

Despite being huge, BIGBANG worries fans might tire of them. "If people start to think 'they've gone bad,' that'll be the moment we stop," admits G-Dragon. "A BIGBANG that isn't fabulous isn't BIGBANG," he added.

ART AND SOUL

Whaddaya know, BIG-BANG's resident work of art, T.O.P, actually

Wow! Happy *Hunger Games*, baby!

collects art himself. His artistic eye is so good that he's curated a number of shows and even wants to open his own museum.

G-Dragon and Taeyang meet ahjussi Karl Lagerfeld.

SPONSOR ME

G-Dragon has more sponsorships than a soccer mom running a 5k, including Hyundai, Nike, Airbnb, Kappa, and fancy-pants fashion house Chanel.

KOREAN WAVE

T.O.P

Full name:
Choi Seung-hyun
Role: Lead rapper,
vocalist, visual

SEUNGRI

Full name:
Lee Seung-hyun
Role: Lead dancer,
vocalist, maknae

G-DRAGON

Full name:
Kwon Ji-yong
Role: Leader, main
rapper, vocalist, face

DAESUNG

Full name:
Kang Dae-sung
Role: Lead vocalist

TAEYANG

Full name:
Dong Young-bae
Role: Main vocalist,
main dancer

SOLO
SUPERSTARS

When idols go solo, you just know it's about to get real.

Bo-A

The queen of K-pop has been killing it for nearly two decades. The closest thing to Korea's Kylie, she's as passionate and driven as she is talented. She also has more hit records than just about anyone—nails emoji.

Eric Nam

GQ Korea's Man of the Year 2016 does it all: a TV personality, presenter, interviewer—but it's as a musician that he excels. The Korean American makes low-key R&B, like Justin Bieber at his most soulful, and "Honestly" is the summer jam everyone needs, whatever the time of year.

G-Dragon

Nothing can stop the success of G-Dragon. Oh, there is something. The one thing that stops all male idols—military service. Kwon Ji-yong is serving in the 3rd Infantry Divison in the Gangwon Province, so fans will have to wait to see what he does next, other than wearing a lot of khaki.

Jennie

With her debut solo single, the aptly-named "Solo," it looks like Jennie is well on the way to a legit world takeover. The BLACKPINK triple threat means business, and whatever she's selling, we're buying. Take cover, Selena, Dua, and Ariana—you've been warned.

CL

On "Doctor Pepper" with Diplo, the 2NE1 diva quenched our thirst, giving as good as Cardi and Nicki. She performed at the 2018 Winter Olympics, and even had a song on the *My Little Pony* soundtrack. What more of an endorsement do you need?

Sunmi

If it had been sung in English by Rita Ora, "Gashina," the third single from Wonder Girls idol Sunmi, could have been a number one record around the world. With tropical beats and whistle chorus, it was a huge hit in Korea, marking her first solo number one there. Surely it's only a matter of time before she has a hit in the West.

HyunA

The controversial singer and rapper likes to break the rules. Whether it's in her sexy videos or by dating her Triple H bandmate E'Dawn, she keeps the Korean public on their toes. And while they're there, she makes sure to keep them up all night dancing to EDM party monsters like "Red" and "Lip and Hip."

8 EYEBROW RAISING

FASHION

These looks are, um, "directional"—yeah, let's go with that.

YUNHO TVXQ

● The Summer Universiade opening ceremony
"Look into my cape of dreams, and one, two, three—you're hypnotized. Now go to the store and buy me some milk, eggs, and trash bags."

BTS

● SBS Awards Festival
The people who grumped about having a female Doctor on *Doctor Who* should brace themselves for the seven Korean Doctors in season 12.

NCT

● Super Seoul Dream Concert
For some, Halloween comes but once a year. For NCT it's, like, alternate Tuesdays.

IU

● Sony headphones launch event
IU is not one of the most beautiful and chic pop stars in Korea—she is a car sponge, okay?

46

MOMENTS

MAMAMOO

○ Showcase for the mini-album *Purple*
Mamamoo set phasers to the opposite of stun in these bootleg Starfleet uniforms.

LEETEUK
SUPER JUNIOR

○ "Sexy, Free and Single" M/V
If Storm from X-Men had a boyfriend called Wind Chill.

JUNG IL-HOON
BTOB

○ "Wow" M/V
There's loads of inspirational style icons: David Beckham, Ryan Gosling, Zayn Malik . . . but Jessie from *Toy Story*'s cool too—you do you, bro.

2NE1

○ MTV Awards Japan
To anyone with 20/20 vision this looks like a collection of Papersource pencil cases.

트와이스

TWICE

Have you succumbed to the talents of TWICE? Yes or yes?

WE LIKEY LIKEY

How do they do it? TWICE are adorable yet in no way annoying. They bring straight-up joy without trying to be edgy, weird, or cool and this surely accounts for their broad appeal and nickname "Asia's number one girl group." Like Little Mix, they were formed through a TV reality show (*Sixteen*)—imagine *that* epic collab!

FIZZY POP

"Color Pop" is a term coined to describe the bright, energetic music that takes you up and down and all around the genre spectrum like a *TWICEcoaster.*

KONICHIWA K-POPULARITY

With three Japanese members: Mina, Sana, and Momo, it's unsurprising that TWICE is the most popular K-pop girl group in Japan. Although K-pop girl groups are not as popular in Japan as they used to be, TWICE is bucking the trend, regularly having number ones and breaking sales records.

M/V QUEENS

With their M/Vs, TWICE creates transportive mini-movies that fans go nuts for. They were the first K-pop band to get 100 million views on YouTube in just 71 days with their single "TT," where the girls dressed as a bunny, pirate, superhero, vampire, ice queen, Pinocchio, mermaid, fairy, and devil. It now has 400+ million views.

2 X FUN

MOMO
Full name: Hirai Momo
Role: Main dancer, vocalist, rapper

JIHYO
Full name: Park Ji-hyo
Role: Leader, main vocalist

NAYEON
Full name: Im Na-yeon
Role: Lead vocalist, lead dancer, center

MINA
Full name: Myoui Mina
Role: Main dancer, vocalist

TZUYU
Full name: Chou Tzu-yu
Role: Lead dancer, vocalist, visual, maknae

JEONGYEON
Full name: Yoo Jung-yeon
Role: Lead vocalist

DAHYUN
Full name: Kim Da-hyun
Role: Lead rapper, vocalist

CHAEYOUNG
Full name: Son Chae-young
Role: Main rapper, vocalist

SANA
Full name: Minatozaki Sana
Role: Vocalist

DANCE MAGIC DANCE

If K-pop is an entire package, then dance is the wrapping, box, and bow.

EXO gives the Easter Bunny a surprising rebrand.

"From the moment I was born, dance was there. Rather than saying that movement and dancing makes me happy, I want to say that my first memories were of dance."
KAI

"I like dances that have a feminine feel, but I also like powerful choreography."
MOMO

POLL STAR

In 2018 Korean news agency Ilgan Sports polled 100 idols including BLACKPINK, GOT7, BTOB, BTS, TWICE, WINNER, EXID, Red Velvet, Wanna One, and SEVENTEEN to find out who they thought were the best dancers in K-pop—and the winners were . . .

1 Kai (EXO) tied with **MOMO (TWICE)** (13 votes)

2 Hoshi (SEVENTEEN) (10 votes)

3 JIMIN (BTS) tied with **TAEMIN (SHINee)** (6 votes)

4 J-HOPE (BTS) tied with **Eunhyuk (Super Junior)** (5 votes)

5 Park Woo-jin (Wanna One) (4 votes)

5 ICONIC DANCE MOVES

1 "Gee" willikers, but Girls' Generation's knock-kneed grandma tears up the floor.

2 Super Junior's iconic "begging pray hands" move proves they're "Sorry," not sorry.

3 In "I Am The Best" by 2NE1, "No, no, no" is delivered through the power of fingers.

4 Hips definitely don't lie for SHINee in the "Ring Ding Dong" routine.

5 TWICE "Cheered Up" everyone and reeled them in with their rope-pulling move.

It's a challenge . . .

If you have any doubt about K-pop idols being absolute beasts when it comes to the get down, watch a few insanely entertaining *Weekly Idol* dance clips on YouTube. Try Jungkook serving a full EXID fantasy, Red Velvet dancing double-time, Lisa (BLACKPINK)'s slayage of TWICE, and Haechan nailing every move in the NCT dance-off.

JINYOUNG

Full name:
Park Jin-young
Role: Lead vocalist,
lead dancer

JB

Full name:
Lim Jae-beom
Role: Leader, main vocalist,
lead dancer, center

MARK

Full name:
Mark Yi-en Tuan
Role: Main rapper,
lead dancer, sub-
vocalist, visual

YUGYEOM

Full name:
Kim Yu-gyeom
Role: Main dancer, lead
vocalist, rapper, maknae

YOUNGJAE

Full name:
Choi Young-jae
Role: Main vocalist

BAMBAM

Full name:
Kunpimook Bhuwakul
Role: Lead rapper, lead dancer,
sub-vocalist

JACKSON

Full name:
Jackson Wang
Role: Lead rapper,
lead dancer, sub-
vocalist, face

갓세븐

GOT7

Stand up if you love pussy bows.

Forget about three—seven is the magic number, 'kay?

GOT GAME

Want to know the band most like BTS that isn't BTS? GOT7. Why? Because they've got seven members, duh. Their rap game is strong, they have a heap of danceable tunes, and they look superb in your grandma's blouse. When JYP launched GOT7 in 2014, they were the company's first boy band in six years, and anticipation was high. Luckily they nailed it. Their latest album, *Present: You*, topped the iTunes album chart in 25 countries and went platinum on the Gaon album chart in less than two months—still GOT it.

ANGLIAPHILES

Two fandoms collided in the spectacular M/V for "Lullaby" in 2018 when Jinyoung was seen flying a car that looked a lot like the blue Ford Anglia Harry and Ron crashed into the Whomping Willow in *Harry Potter and the Chamber of Secrets*. Magic FM.

KING OF K-POP?

First Jackson Wang won the Teen Choice Award for Next Big Thing, then he released "Different Game" with Gucci Mane. Stardom is surely on the horizon.

BA-BAM!

BamBam's nickname came from '60s cartoon *The Flintstones*. Bambam was a white-haired toddler who bashed things with a giant club. Hmmmm?

THE LANGUAGE OF SLEEP

The boys recorded Korean, Chinese, English, and Spanish versions of their single "Lullaby," meaning that a huge chunk of the world will be able to understand them. Don't worry, Belgium—your time will come.

TUCKERED OUT

53

WHEN K-POP GETS HOT

Idols kiss goodbye to their Goody-Two-shoes image . . . ever so slightly.

 Shake Jibooty

Jimin fills out red chinos better than anyone since Louis Tomlinson, and it has not gone unnoticed: all hail the "Jibooty."

War of Hormone in action right there

 Pepero kiss game

Koreans aren't keen on overt displays of intimacy, but there are some tricks to get around that, one being: the Pepero Kiss Game where friends dare themselves to share a stick, leading to a peck on the lips. The person with the shortest bit of breadstick wins. Fans go all sorts of cray for this, with YouTube video views in the millions.

Yura Girl's Day and Hong Jong-hyun play the game on TV show _We Got Married_.

 **Man's struggle with his shirt**

Maybe Jungkook's clothes are too itchy because, whether he's performing onstage or in M/Vs like "Fake Love," he always seems to be trying to pull his shirt off, and it's not just him—a lot of boy banders suffer from this debiltating affliction. Brrrrrr.

 **Shipping**

Shipping is the uncontrollable desire for your fave idols to hook up, regardless of gender, often based on perceived chemistry or cute visuals. Popular "ships" are VKook (Jungkook and V from BTS), HunHan (Luhan and Sehun from EXO), and Marksana (Sana from TWICE and Mark from GOT7).

 **Gay idol**

K-pop's first "out" gay singer, Holland, racked up 300,000 votes to come in first in 2018's _Dazed 100_ poll—a list that predicts the artists that'll shape the future. His dreamy M/V for "Neverland" has had 10+ million views.

What would Mom say?

🔥 NSFW M/Vs

Always on the edge of risqué, Jay Park's "MOMMAE" was A LOT, and with a 19+ rating was effectively banned from TV.

🔥 Sweary Mary

Maybe they lose something in translation, but to English speakers, songs like Gain's "Fxxx U" (featuring Bumkey) are a bit of a shock. It sounds pretty darn jaunty until you get to that four-letter chorus, and then there's the controversial M/V: wow!

Wanna One hugs it out on KBS variety show *Happy Together.*

🔥 Fan service

Anything you do to get a specific reaction from your fans is fan service. This includes everything from aegyo to calculated displays of skin and skinship. Dancing dripping wet like EXO's Kai and Sehun did at their jaw-dropping SBS Gayo Daejeon Music Festival performance works, too.

Forget your umbrellas again, guys?

🔥 Skinship

When band-mates hug each other, grab, or playfight, that's skinship. It's basically an outward display of emotional kinship with your bandmate, where you may or may not make skin contact. Koreans can be very affectionate. Awww together now!

WORLD IDOL

Not all K-pop idols are from South Korea, you know?

CANADA
- **Henry Lau (Super Junior)** was born in Toronto.
- **Mark (NCT Dream)** is from Vancouver.
- **Wendy** grew up in South Korea but moved to Canada when she was about 10. She later moved to America.

UK
- Solo K-pop singer **Shannon** has a Welsh dad and Korean mom, and went to school in London.

CHINA
- **Lay (EXO)**
- **Zhou Mi (Super Junior-M)** was born in Wuhan.

JAPAN
- **Mina, Momo, and Sana** from **TWICE** are all Japanese.
- **Yuta (NCT 127)** is from Osaka.
- **Yuto (Pentagon)**

SOUTH KOREA

US
- **Amber (f(x))** is Californian of Taiwanese descent.
- **Nichkhun (2PM)** was born in Cali.
- **Eric Nam** is from Atlanta, Georgia.
- **Mark (GOT7)** is of Taiwanese descent, but grew up in LA.

THAILAND
- **Lisa (BLACKPINK)** calls Bangkok home.
- **BamBam (GOT7)**
- **Ten (NCT)** was born in Thailand but has Chinese heritage.
- **Sorn (CLC)**

HONG KONG
- **Jackson Wang (GOT7)**

TAIWAN
- **Tzuyu (TWICE)**
- **Kuanlin (Wanna One)** was born in Taipei.

NEW ZEALAND
- **Rosé (BLACKPINK)** is a Kiwi by birth and spent most of her childhood in Australia before moving to South Korea.

TEMPORARY IDOLS

Success, sadly for fans, does not guarantee stability.

Project groups have become a big thing in South Korea and not everyone is happy about it. TV shows are taking trainees from entertainment companies and making them audition for spots in a group, a bit like *The X Factor,* but the groups are only temporary platforms for the members to showcase their talent, before they return to their original company.

WANNA ONE

Wanna One was launched on season two of *Produce 101* in 2017, but they became so massively popular, fans didn't want them to split up. The band, which was put together by the public, became superstars overnight, coming in at number two on the 2018 *Forbes* list of most powerful celebrities in Korea, just behind BTS. Wannable 4EVA.

IZ*ONE

I.O.I

Twelve-piece girl group IZ*ONE were put together for the show *Produce 48*, and when they launched their mega-catchy first single "La Vie en Rose" on October 29, 2018, it became an instant classic, gaining over four million YouTube views in 24 hours.

When I.O.I, the girl group launched via the first series of *Produce 101*, released songs like "Very Very Very," they did VERY well, but their post-break-up careers have failed to meet expectations.

YERI
Full name:
Kim Ye-rim
Role: Sub vocal, sub-rapper, maknae

SEULGI
Full name:
Kang Seul-gi
Role: Main dancer, lead vocal

JOY
Full name:
Park Soo-young
Role: Lead rapper, vocalist

IRENE
Full name:
Bae Joo-hyun
Role: Leader, main rapper, lead dancer, visual, center, vocalist

WENDY
Full name:
Shon Seung-wan
Role: Main vocal

RED VELVET

Sweet—with none of the calories.

SEEING RED

SM Entertainment launched Red Velvet in 2014 as a quirky quartet, but maknae Yeri joined in 2015 and they never looked back. Their infectious first single "Happiness" was written by

Chad Hugo, one half of Grammy-winning production super-team the Neptunes (the other half is Pharrell Williams). Their songs are pure joy even when Joy isn't rapping, the M/Vs are nutty as an ice cream cake and the aesthetic is 100% summer magic.

NOT SO DUMB

"Dumb Dumb" was voted the best K-pop song

of 2015 by *Dazed*, while the kooky M/V was classed as one of the best of the year by *Rolling Stone*.

STANS IN HIGH PLACES

Red Velvet are one of the few idol groups to ever perform in North Korea. Its leader, Kim Jong-un, who watched the show, is said to be a fan. Wonder if he has an ultimate bias.

TOTAL LEGEND

In October 2018, Wendy joined the likes of Sam Smith and Ariana Grande by duetting with John Legend. The slinky English language ballad "Written in the Stars,"

with its cinema noir mini-movie M/V, is 100% velvet.

2 BECOME 1

Red Velvet introduced K-pop fans to the dual aspect identity through their name. *Red* highlights their bright, bouncy side, *Velvet* represents sophisticated R&B. Without them, we might not have had BLACKPINK, who use the same principles.

BLAZER GLORY

RED VELVET

"I always write down how I feel about myself. I used to keep a diary, but these days I make short notes." **Wonder what Irene writes to herself: be more perfect?**

"My dream is to have our Red Velvet concert overseas, one day. I hope. Maybe in 15 years, 20 years." **You're joking, right Wendy? Get here NOW!**

"I learned that worrying about something doesn't solve the problem. I'm going to try to live simpler and more fun."
Live like Seulgi: no worries.

"Although I usually play and joke around with the members, I become the opposite during the recording sessions. While waiting for my turn at the studio, I focus and listen to the music."
Yeri takes a break from being the evil maknae.

"We talk all night long and we don't sleep much."
Joy explains what life living with Red Velvet is like. Sleepover anyone?

20 K-POP SONGS

to stream now

A mixtape of solid-gold K-classics

1

Wonder Girls, "Tell Me" (2007)
This Casio bop sounded like a freestyle Stacey Q, 1980s fhrowback even in 2007.

2

Brown Eyed Girls, "Abracadabra" (2009)
The magic here is that this dirty vocoder jam still sounds so lit.

3

Super Junior, "Sorry, Sorry" (2009)
Let's play a love game . . . how much do SJ stan Lady Gaga?

4

SHINee, "Lucifer" (2010)
Hellishly catchy explosion of synth stabs and staccato robo-harmonies.

5

Girl's Day, "Nothing Lasts Up" (2010)
Keep telling yourself that this is not a Spice Girls song.

6

2NE1, "I Am the Best" (2011)
A swarm of funky rave hornets nesting in M.I.A.'s basement bring all the boys to the yard.

7

INFINITE, "The Chaser" (2012)
A glorious and soaring electro panic attack that could easily win *Idol*.

8

BIGBANG, "Fantastic Baby" (2012)
This EDM banger was featured on *Glee* back in 2012. I-CON-IC.

9

**Girls' Generation,
"I Got a Boy"** (2013)
Four songs spliced together to make K-pop perfection. MEGA.

10

**Orange Caramel,
"Catallena"** (2014)
Could easily be a lost Boney M. track—a good thing, no, really!

11

TWICE, "TT" (2016)
"TT" represents the cry emoji, so how does this pulsing bubblegum joy give such life?

12

**BTS, "Blood Sweat
and Tears"** (2016)
BTS takes flight like an eagle high on tropical surges of emo.

13

**Cosmic Girls (WJSN),
"Secret"** (2016)
This has all the feels. Listen and watch your cares melt away.

14

EXO, "Monster" (2016)
Epic is the only way to describe this crunching monster of whomping squelch pop.

15

Wanna One, "Energetic" (2017)
Straight up does what it says in the title. An energetic dance floor romp. Wanna bop?

16

**Red Velvet,
"Red Flavor"** (2017)
In-your-face chant that doubles as a clarion call for all of K-pop.

17

**MOMOLAND,
"BBoom BBoom"** (2018)
Stupidly catchy, trumpety earworm verging on novelty.

18

**LOONA/yyxy feat. Grimes,
"Love4eva"** (2018)
Sonic the Hedgehog's Chemical Plant Zone got cuter.

19

**BLACKPINK,
"Ddu-Du Ddu-Du"** (2018)
A split personality of swagger and sweetness = major drama.

20

NCT 127, "Regular" (2018)
East meets West via a South American street party in this rhythmic K-Latin fusion.

CREDITS